SUGGESTIONS FOR G

1. **THE ROOM** Discourage people from sit[...] circle – all need to be equally involved.

2. **HOSPITALITY** Tea or coffee on arrival c[...] Perhaps at the end too, to encourage peop[...] might be more ambitious, taking it in turns to bring a dessert to [...] evening (even in Lent, hospitality is OK!) with coffee at the end.

3. **THE START** If group members don't know each other well, some kind of 'icebreaker' might be helpful. For example, you might invite people to share something quite secular (where they grew up, holidays, hobbies, etc.). Place a time limit on this exercise.

4. **PREPARING THE GROUP** Take the group into your confidence, e.g. 'I've never done this before', or 'I've led lots of groups and each one has contained surprises'. Sharing vulnerability is designed to encourage all members to see the success of the group as their responsibility. Ask those who know that they talk easily to ration their contributions, and encourage the reticent to speak at least once or twice – however briefly. Explain that there are no 'right' answers and that among friends it is fine to say things that you are not sure about – to express half-formed ideas. However, if individuals choose to say nothing, that's all right too.

5. **THE MATERIAL** Encourage members to read next time's session *before* the meeting. It helps enormously if each group member has their own personal copy of this booklet (so the price is reduced either when multiple copies are ordered or if you order online). *There is no need to consider all the questions.* A lively exchange of views is what matters, so be selective. You can always spread a session over two or more meetings, if you run out of time!

   For some questions you might start with a few minutes' silence to make jottings. Or you might ask members to talk in sub-groups of two or three, before sharing with the whole group.

6. **PREPARATION** Decide beforehand whether to distribute (or ask people to bring) paper, pencils, hymn books, etc. If possible, ask people in advance to read a Bible passage or lead in prayer, so that they can prepare.

7. **TIMING** Try to start on time and make sure you stick fairly closely to your stated finishing time.

8. **USING THE CD/AUDIOTAPE** Some groups will play the 14-minute piece at the beginning of the meeting. Other groups will prefer to play it at the end – or to play 7/8 minutes at the beginning and the rest halfway through the meeting. The track markers (on the CD only) will help you find any section very easily, including the Closing Reflections, which you may wish to play again at the end of the session.

   You can ignore these markers altogether, of course, if you prefer.

SESSION 1

YORK COURSES

WHEN I SURVEY...
Christ's cross and ours

A course in five sessions
written by John Pridmore
Accompanying CD-tape and transcript available

DARKNESS AT NOON

The story of Jesus is not a story of intolerance towards a progressive young man, which a little education and kindness of heart would have amended – it is God who is on the cross.

Dorothy L. Sayers

Love. The power of love... Love not just as a sentiment, but as a strategy. Through the ultimate sacrifice of his life – death on the cross – he transformed that cross from an instrument of the most horrendous torture to a tool for liberation – eternal freedom. Jesus Christ our Saviour.

Paul Boateng

When I was a school chaplain I used to try to explain to my confirmation classes what the cross means. Lord have mercy on me, I used to try to *explain*. These days I'm less confident in explanations. Better not to explain, but to stay as long as we can beneath the cross – and then to stay there a little longer.

We met in a little 'upper room' in my house. In the centre of the room was a big round low table with a white surface. We'd all sit on cushions on the floor around this table. And I'd give everyone a felt-tip pen, a 'magic marker'. Then I'd invite these young people to write all over the table. (Needless to say, these were water-based pens!) I'd invite them to write down anything and everything that made them unhappy or ashamed. I'd ask them to write down what saddened them about their world or – if they wanted to – about their own lives. Then I would invite them to imagine that table as being as big as the great round world – indeed as being so big that it reached as far as the beginning and the end of time.

Then I would invite them to think of all that they had written on the table as funnelling in, as coming together and bearing down on one point at the very centre of the table.

The crossroads of history

And then we thought of one place, one person, and one moment at the mid-point of history. We thought of Christ's cross. We would picture that crucified figure, absorbing the shame and the pain of all we had written on the table. We thought of that one lonely figure carrying – and carrying away – all the sins and sorrows of our sad human story. Christ's cross – and ours.

The Gospels prefer pictures to explanations. One picture they give us is of *darkness* descending. We read that on 'Good Friday', as we call it, there was 'darkness over the whole land' (Mark 15.33). It is night at noon. These were not sudden storm clouds. The Gospels show no interest in the weather. Darkness in the Gospels, as throughout our Bible, signifies all that defies the purpose of God, all that spurns the love of God, all that contradicts the Creator's command, 'Let there be light'.

So at the cross all the wretchedness and misery of our long story; all our pain and folly; all evil things of flesh, of speech, of spirit; all that was surely never meant to be, bear down on this broken man.

The cry of dereliction

Then, out of the darkness, there is a single terrible cry, a cry so anguished that they remembered the very Aramaic in which the words were uttered, *Eloi, eloi, lama sabachthani?* 'My God, my God, why have you forsaken me?' (Mark 15.34). The one with whom Jesus had walked, whom he had dared call '*Abba*, Father', is no longer there. This is the cup Jesus prayed he would never have to drink. This is 'the inner crucifixion' of the Son of God.

What is going on?

We dare to say this. What evil does is to divide. Evil pulls apart what belongs together. That is true of our petty little quarrels, the silly spats that divide individuals one from another. It is true as well of the conflicts between races and nations. Evil separates. And so we have our family rows – teenagers storming out of the room – and our world wars.

We believe that Jesus, in some way beyond our comprehension, made our sins and sorrows his own. Evil divides. Sin tears apart. The worst separation Jesus could possibly suffer was to lose the sense of his Father with him. And this separation he suffers. This final alienation, too, he makes his own. Jesus takes into himself the worst we know, including that ultimate loneliness when even God himself seems to go. He makes that darkness his own.

The crucified God

But we must say something else, however paradoxical and contradictory it sounds. We dare to say that on his cross, as at every step of his way, '*God* was in Christ'. This is how St Paul put it – 'God was in Christ reconciling the world to himself' (2 Corinthians 5.19). We dare to say God had not gone. God knows what it is to be abandoned by God – though our words fall apart as we try to speak of these things. 'God goes where God is not, so that what is not God may be drawn into the eternal love' (*Hans Urs von Balthasar*).

Perhaps only the saints understand. I think of someone I met just once. When those who knew her well talked about her, they tended to use images of light. They spoke of her radiance. They spoke of her as 'a shining light'. It was as if she reflected a light too great for most of us to bear. You could see it in her eyes, they said. From my one brief meeting with her, I'll vouch for that.

And yet, and yet... Mother Teresa of Calcutta spent the last thirty years of her life, feeling her way as best she could through a deep inner darkness. We know this from letters from her that have now been published. She writes to her Archbishop, 'Please pray for me – the longing for God is terribly painful and yet the darkness is becoming greater. What contradiction there is in my soul – the pain within is so great... Please ask Our Lady to be my Mother in this darkness.'

Dealing with our darkness

What of our own darkness? Many of us, who would never presume to be bracketed with Mother Teresa, have nevertheless known something of the darkness when God seems to go. My friend Peter was a priest. He was one of the finest Christians I've known. He made Jesus real to me, as he did to the people of his parish. But Peter told me before he died that often he'd go for months feeling that God had abandoned him.

How can we describe that darkness? We talk about 'the darkness *before* dawn'. This is more like the darkness we sometimes feel *at* dawn, when just getting up to face a new day can be very hard. The poet Gerard Manley Hopkins wrote glorious joyful poetry. 'Glory be to God for dappled things!' he sang. But for Hopkins, as for Mother Teresa, for much of the time, it was inwardly very dark. 'I wake and feel the fell of dark, not day,' he wrote.

What can we do about our darkness? I find it helpful simply to keep on saying just six words from the Psalms: 'He made darkness his secret place' (Psalm 18.11). A daring and haunting line from another poet, Henry Vaughan, suggests that darkness is an aspect of the divine. 'There is in God, some say, a deep but dazzling darkness'.

All in the waiting

And it's sensible to wait. In fact, it's essential to wait. With the hymn-writer James Montgomery, we pray for 'patience to watch, and wait, and weep, though mercy long delay'. The poet T S Eliot, too, believed that the best thing to do when things are dark is to wait.

> I said to my soul, be still, and wait without hope
> For hope would be hope for the wrong thing;
> wait without love
> For love would be love of the wrong thing;
> there is yet faith

But the faith and the love and the hope are
    all in the waiting.
Wait without thought, for you are not ready
    for thought:
So the darkness shall be the light, and the
    stillness the dancing.

('East Coker', *Four Quartets*)

'The darkness shall be the light'. When Jesus cried from the cross, 'My God, my God, why have you forsaken me?' he was quoting from a psalm (Psalm 22.1). Rabbi Hugo Gryn, who survived Auschwitz, loved the psalms. He believed that the opening line of a psalm encapsulates the whole psalm. Psalm 22 opens with a cry of dereliction, but it ends on a note of hope. Nothing can diminish the sense of utter abandonment voiced by Jesus. But this terrible cry will not be his last word from the cross.

Picture for Session 3

QUESTIONS FOR GROUPS
BIBLE READING: Mark 15.33–38

1. The Gospels record seven sayings of Jesus from the cross. How many can you remember? (You'll find a complete list on pages 7-8.) How many are hopeful/practical/sad? Which sayings 'speak' to you most directly?

2. One church hit the headlines when it decided to remove a large crucifix from an outside wall, on the grounds that the figure of a man dying in agony frightened the local children. Church members wanted to replace it with an empty cross – a sign of resurrection. What do you think of this decision?

3. In Holy Week an interested but unconvinced friend asks, 'What does Christ's death on the cross mean to you?' How would you explain?

4. *Read Romans 5.1-5.* With the cross as its central symbol, Christianity can appear gloomy. Yet the New Testament stresses 'joy' and 'peace', and research suggests that faith often generates personal happiness. How does your experience of life relate to this wide spectrum of emotions?

5. *Read Psalm 13.* Some Christians experience 'the dark night of the soul'. Mother Teresa did (see page 4). Does this make her more, or less, holy, in your view?

6. Do group members have experience of darkness or desolation? If so, how did/do they cope with this?

7. A mother whose baby died said that the words of Jesus ('My God, my God, why have you forsaken me?') brought her comfort. It was, for her, a statement of faith in desolate times. She knew that Jesus understood what she was living through. Does your experience of life help you understand this attitude?

8. *Read John 8.12.* Can you identify 'dark places' and places blazing with light in our Nation's life and in the Church's life (both national and local)? 'It is better to light a candle than to curse the darkness.' Can you give examples of people (famous and/or just local) who have 'lit a candle'.

9. *Read Matthew 5.14-16.* Jesus looked at that unlikely group of disciples and half-disciples gathered on the hillside and said, 'You are the light of the world'. What implications does this have for you as an individual/a group/a church?

10. *Read Ephesians 2.13-22.* Read the two paragraphs on page 3 beginning: 'We dare to say this'. Share examples of division and reconciliation known to you – domestic or international. What lessons for life have these taught you?

11. To end on an upbeat note... reflect on the responses to Simon Stanley's final question about coping with dark times (Track [10] on the course CD/transcript). Discuss the participants' insights and share your own.

12. As a group, you might wish to try the exercise described at the beginning of this session. (If a big round low white table with a white surface is not available, a large sheet of 'ceiling paper' will do!)

To close the session you might like to keep silence and then say the lovely and well-known prayer on page 5.

SESSION 2

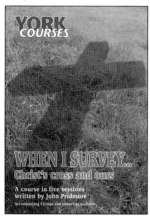

Into Great Silence

The film opened 'to rapturous acclaim across the Western world'. 'It has been a phenomenal box office smash-hit.' So says the slip-case that the DVD comes in. This is not the latest Hollywood blockbuster, nor is it the latest James Bond or Harry Potter. No, this film, which has had such astonishing universal appeal, is a documentary, nearly three hours long, recording life inside a Trappist monastery.

The monastery is set high in the French Alps. In this breathtakingly beautiful but chilling and inhospitable landscape, the monks spend their days, indeed their whole lives, almost entirely in silence. The film is silent too, apart from the chants we hear from the great abbey church. In its English version, the film is entitled *Into Great Silence*.

The thirst for silence

How do we account for the success of this film? I believe that it appeals to us as much as it does because, deep within us, there is a thirst for silence. Paradoxically, this is a thirst of which we are not always aware. We are told that those who are dehydrated do not always feel thirsty. So it is with our need for silence.

We talk and talk, whether or not we have anything to say. Every day we exchange a billion emails. By the laws of natural selection, the mobile phone will soon be part of the human anatomy. I shudder to think of all the sermons that have been preached since Christianity was born! Seeing the film *Into Great Silence*, awakens us to our thirst for silence. It makes us realise our need to shut up and be still.

When we come to the cross we enter, with Jesus, 'into great silence'.

Jesus is silent before those who accuse him and who torture him. He is silent before the orchestrated demands for his death coming from the crowds. He is silent before Herod. He is silent before Pilate. To be sure, St John in his Gospel, reflecting later on what it all means, does have Jesus conversing with Pilate. But, once sentence is passed on him, in John's account too, Jesus falls silent.

On the cross, Jesus enters 'into great silence'. According to Matthew and Mark that silence is broken just once – by that single terrible utterance, 'My God, my God, why have you forsaken me?' (Mark 15.34; Matthew 27.46). Luke in his Gospel has his three 'sayings from the cross'. Jesus asks his father to forgive his executioners (Luke 23.34). He promises paradise to the penitent thief (Luke 23.43). And, as he dies, he commends his spirit to his father (Luke 23.46). John too records three sayings. Jesus commends his mother to his beloved disciple (John 19.26–27). He cries, 'I thirst' (John 19.28) and, at the last, triumphantly, 'It is finished' (John 19.30).

We often meditate on these words. In many churches, these 'seven words from the cross' provide the theme for the traditional three-hour service on Good Friday. It is to our profit that we think deeply about what Jesus says before he dies. Crucifixion made *breathing* an agony, let alone speaking. Every last word, uttered in such pain, demands our attention. But those seven sayings are all we hear, save for one last terrible cry. The rest is silence.

The silence of the lamb

Four hundred years or so before the time of Jesus, a prophet who was also a poet, spoke of a 'servant' who would one day suffer to set God's people free. This servant, the prophet said, would bear the people's sins and share their sorrows. And he would do so *silently*. 'He was oppressed and afflicted,' says this prophet, 'yet he did not open his mouth; he was led like a lamb to the slaughter, and as a sheep before her shearers is dumb, so he did not open his mouth' (Isaiah 53.7). As we read these words, we are bound to think of 'the great silence' of Jesus. When we ponder Christ's silence, we begin to be ashamed of our noise.

Jesus had sought silence long before he entered 'the great silence' of Good Friday. When he wanted to be especially close to God, Jesus withdrew to the desert. Not that the desert is ever exactly silent. The desert has many voices. It is never quite still, even when there is no breath of wind to disturb the sands. When nothing is to be heard, as all who have travelled in the desert will testify, the very silence becomes audible and eloquent.

T E Lawrence, 'Lawrence of Arabia', was haunted by that silence. The prophet Elijah, who, in fear of his life, hid in a cave in the back of beyond, heard it too. The older translations of the Bible say that, after a fire had swept the mountainside and an earthquake had made the ground tremble, Elijah heard 'a still small voice' (1 Kings 19.12). But the original Hebrew words might just as well be translated as 'the sound of silence'. And in that silence God spoke.

Without a word

'Be still,' says the psalmist 'and know that I am God' (Psalm 46.10). We should cherish 'the sound of silence', for it can become the voice of God within. Surely we talk too much. We hear the command to preach the gospel and we take it as a licence to lecture without listening.

We read what Peter says: 'Be ready always to give an answer to everyone who asks you a reason for the hope that is in you' (1 Peter 3.15). But we fail to notice what he says next – that our answers should be given 'with meekness and fear'. And we may have missed what he has already said – in what, to be sure, is a highly contentious passage – about unbelieving husbands. Wives may win them over 'without a word'! (1 Peter 3.1-2)

One of the striking features of the story of Jesus is that he sometimes told people to keep quiet about him. For example, when Jesus raised Jairus's daughter from the dead – a tale we love to tell – he left the family with two instructions. He ordered that the little girl should be given something to eat – but he also insisted that no one should know what he had done (Mark 5.43).

Quiet Christianity

We sing the hymn, *We have a gospel to proclaim* – and indeed we do have such a gospel. But then we reflect on 'the great silence' of Jesus, and we remember how adamant Jesus was that there are occasions when it is best not to say anything. Then we recognise that perhaps there needs to be a 'Christian pause button'!

If faith lacks conviction, it is unpersuasive. But if faith is strident, it does not ring true. 'Quiet Christianity' isn't a contradiction in terms. Quiet Christianity respects the fundamental mystery of things. Quiet Christianity does not always try to explain, but simply watches and waits beneath the cross, echoing in its own heart the anguished 'Why?' of the One who hangs there. Quiet Christianity reaches into the great silence of the crucified Jesus. That is the vocation of the monk and the nun committed to the silent quest for God, knowing that where words cease, there God is to be found.

Outside monasteries, there is little silence left in our world, but to save our souls alive we must seek it.

Aberfan

At 9.15 a.m. on Friday, 21 October, 1966 a waste tip slid down a mountain into the mining village of Aberfan in

> Perhaps we need a spirituality not so dependent on silence. Perhaps we need sharper expectations of behaviour for all, including children. Or perhaps just a little of both.
>
> *Canon Giles Fraser*

South Wales. In its path was Pantglas Junior School. The children had just returned to their classes after assembly when the tide of waste engulfed their school. One hundred and sixteen children died, together with five of their teachers. The hymn they had sung in assembly was *All things bright and beautiful.*

I was a curate at the time, attached to a church in Cornwall. That appalling tragedy happened on the Friday. I remember my sense of relief that I wasn't preaching on Sunday. Two other clergy were down to preach, one at the morning service, the other in the evening. More than forty years later, I remember their sermons. Both my colleagues talked about what had happened in Aberfan. But their two sermons were very different. The preacher in the morning took as his text the words 'Unless you repent, you too will all perish!' (Luke 13.3–5). He preached at length. He claimed that what had happened to the children of Aberfan was God's warning to us and that much the same terrible punishment will fall on the unrepentant.

The sermon in the evening was delivered far less confidently. I cannot recall much of what the preacher said, simply because he could not find much to say. There were long pauses. He struggled for words, but words failed him, and finally he fell silent.

Sometimes we must do so, too.

Prayers from the Christians of Korea / Week of Prayer for Christian Unity 2009

Prayer of Acclamation and Commitment

Leader: Blessed are you O Christ:
All: When we are without hope your cross is our hope.

Leader: Blessed are you O Christ:
All: When we are lost your cross is our guide.

Leader: Blessed are you O Christ:
All: When we are blind your cross is our light.

Leader: Blessed are you O Christ:
All: When we are weak your cross is our power.

Leader: Blessed are you O Christ:
All: When we are oppressed your cross sets us free.

Leader: Blessed are you O Christ:
All: When we are in peril your cross is our peace.

Leader: Blessed are you O Christ:
All: When we are apart your cross unites.

Leader: God of all the world:
All: We are united in your Cross.
In you, O Christ, is love and your love has set us free.

QUESTIONS FOR GROUPS

BIBLE READING: Isaiah 53.1–7

1. **Read Ecclesiastes 3.7** and **James 3.3–6.** Can you describe an occasion when you wish you'd kept silent – and when you regret not speaking up for someone else, for yourself, or for your beliefs? John Bell's comment might be helpful here (track [19] on the CD/transcript).

2. **Read Luke 23.8–12** and **Isaiah 53.7.** Jesus was a brilliant orator, yet he chose not to defend himself at his trials. Should Christians never be assertive? How does being assertive differ from being aggressive?

3. **Read Ecclesiastes 5.1–3.** When Quakers meet for worship, they simply sit in silence until someone feels moved to speak. What might we learn from Quaker worship? If a member has experience of this, please share with the group.

4. **Read Psalm 95.1–2.** Exuberant, often noisy, Charismatic/Pentecostal worship is growing faster than any other style of worship across the world. What might we learn from this?

5. A single woman was invited to a silent retreat. Busy people enjoyed it, but she didn't. She said, 'I spend my time in enforced silence; what I need is lively conversation and laughter.' Is it a question of 'horses for courses'? How do group members balance the need for silence/solitude and company/friendship?

6. **Read Mark 5.21–24** and **35–43.** Imagine you are one of the family, bursting to tell everyone. Yet Jesus instructs you to keep quiet. Why do you think he did that?

7. Listen again to the words of Pastor Martin Niemöller on the audiotape or CD (track [15]) or read them in the transcript. Who should the Christian Church be speaking up for today?

8. Read the William Penn box on page 7. Are you aware of a need for silence in your own life? Do you always find silence restful? Do you believe that a need for silence is universal? Or is it a function of our age, our temperament, culture, gender...?

9. How do you/how might you build silence into your life? What competes for this space – family, music, radio, television...?

10. Do you find that solitary silence leads you closer to God? Do you find that shared silence draws you close to God and other people? Do you find that singing and laughter draw you close to God and other people?

11. In the UK there are some 9 million deaf and hard of hearing people. Imagine that you are losing your hearing – how might you cope with such enforced silence and social isolation?

12. Was General Dannatt right to speak out in public, in your view? (Track [18] on CD/transcript).

13. **Read Psalm 46.10.** As a group, sit in silence for 5 minutes. If you wish, share how you felt about the experience.

O God, give me strength...
O guide my spirit,
O raise me from these dark depths...
For you alone understand and can inspire me.

Ludwig van Beethoven

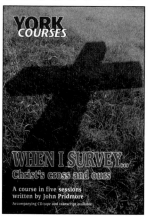

YORK
COURSES

WHEN I SURVEY...
Christ's cross and ours

A course in five sessions
written by John Pridmore
Accompanying CD-tape and transcript available

THE CHILD ON THE CROSS

Grief is the price we pay for love.
HM The Queen
(after 9/11)

Lord, give to men who are old and tougher,

The things that little children suffer.

John Masefield,
The Everlasting Mercy

The cry for God's kingdom to please come and remove the evil that happens in the world is never more intense than when one is looking into the face of a suffering child.

Adrian Warnock

There was a toddler at my feet. He was treating me like a tree. I was fun to climb. Eventually he reached my arms where he settled comfortably and in total trust. Only then did I notice that he was blind. This was in Calcutta, in Shishu Bhavan, the home for abandoned children founded by Mother Teresa.

Why was that little boy blind? He had lost his sight because of a disease. He had caught that disease because he had not had enough food, or the right food. And yet this little boy was relatively lucky. He was lucky to have survived. And lucky to have found a safe and loving home – a home where he would be helped to overcome his disability; a home which would give him the prospect of leading a useful happy life.

Not all children are so lucky.

The state of the world's children

Each year the United Nations Children's Fund (UNICEF) publishes a report, *The State of the World's Children*. Here are a few sentences from the 2008 report:

What is a life worth? Most of us would sacrifice a great deal to save a single child. Yet somehow on a global scale our priorities have become blurred. Every day, on average more than 26,000 children under the age of 5 die around the world, mostly from preventable diseases.

Here are a few more dry statistics. Since 1990 over 2,000,000 children have been killed and 6,000,000 seriously injured in wars. Some 180,000,000 children round the world are used as cheap labour. Around 14,000,000 children under 15 have lost one or both parents to AIDS.

But these big numbers, with their many noughts, hardly touch us. It is the single image that moves us. Three images haunt me. The first two are factual. The third is fictional.

- The first image is of a nameless newborn baby girl. She has been dumped in a Delhi station toilet, discarded simply because she's female.
- The second image is of Pintu. Pintu works in a tannery where they make the leather that goes to manufacturing cricket balls. There Pintu squats all day, surrounded by piles of stinking cattle flesh. And he is not paid a penny. He is a twenty-first-century slave.
- The third image is of a child torn to death by dogs. We read of this child in Dostoevsky's great novel

YORK COURSES

...bring leading Christian thinkers into your discussion groups

NEW COURSE

WHEN I SURVEY...
Christ's cross and ours

with *General Sir Richard Dannatt, John Bell, Christina Baxter. Introduced by Dr David Hope. Closing Reflections by Colin Morris. Course booklet written by the Revd Dr John Pridmore.*

FIVE SESSIONS: Darkness at Noon; Into Great Silence; The Child on the Cross; Outside a City Wall; Touching the Rock

The death of Christ is a dominant and dramatic theme in the New Testament. So it's not surprising that, over the centuries, the Cross has become *the* symbol of the Christian faith. But Christians do not honour a dead hero; we worship a Living Lord.

According to the Bible, the death of Jesus is not the end of a track – it's the gateway into life. His crucifixion gives rise to many key themes and you'll explore some of these in this course including: the place of silence in our noisy world; despair and hope; a suffering world; the challenge of living as disciples when Christianity is no longer mainstream ...

PRICES FOR OUR COURSES

BOOKLET: £3.50 (*£2.99 each for* 5 *or more*)
CD: £10.99 (*£8.99 each for* 2 *or more*)
AUDIOTAPE: £8.99 (*£6.99 each for* 5 *or more*)
TRANSCRIPT: £4.99 (*£2.99 each for* 2 *or more*)
CD TASTER PACK: £15.99
(*1 booklet, 1 CD, 1 transcript*)
worth £19.48 – save £3.49

SPECIAL OFFERS and DISCOUNTS at
www.yorkcourses.co.uk

FREE PACKING and 2nd CLASS POSTAGE
WITHIN THE UK

Each group needs 1 CD or audiotape, plus a course booklet for each member. In addition many groups find the transcript booklet extremely helpful. The COURSE BOOKLET has five chapters, each with questions aimed at provoking wide-ranging discussion. The COURSE CD (or audiotape) consists of five sessions of approximately 14 minutes each, in the style of a radio programme, during which each participant contributes. The words as spoken on the CD/audiotape for the course are set out in the TRANSCRIPT – ideal for group leaders when preparing. It also cross-references with the track numbers on the CD – making it simple to find the start of each new question posed to the participants.

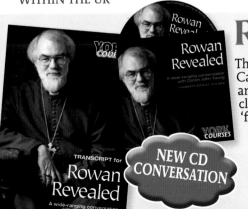

TRANSCRIPT for Rowan Revealed
A wide-ranging conversation with Canon John Young

NEW CD CONVERSATION

Rowan Revealed

The Archbishop of Canterbury talks frankly to Canon John Young of York Courses about his life and faith, prayer, poetry, the press, politics (including the war in Iraq), the future of the Church, 'fresh expressions', what Jesus means to him ...

1 *Rowan Revealed* CD	£5.00
Multipack of **5** CDs	£10.00
Multipack of **25** CDs	£25.00
Rowan Revealed transcript	£2.99

OUR EASY-TO-USE COURSES FOR GROUP DISCUSS

These three...
FAITH, HOPE and LOVE

FIVE SESSIONS: Believing and trusting; The Peace of God; Faith into Love; The Greatest of these; All shall be well

Based on the three great qualities celebrated in 1 Corinthians 13. This famous passage begins and ends in majestic prose. But the middle paragraph is practical and demanding. St Paul's thirteen verses take us to the heart of what it means to be a Christian.

with **Bishop Tom Wright, Anne Atkins, The Abbot of Worth. Professor Frances Young.** *Introduced by* **Dr David Hope**

THE LORD'S PRAYER
praying it, meaning it, living it

FIVE SESSIONS: Our Father; Thy will be done; Our daily bread; As we forgive; In heaven

In the Lord's Prayer Jesus gives us a pattern for living as his disciples. This famous prayer also raises vital questions for today's world in which 'daily bread' is uncertain for billions and a refusal to 'forgive those who trespass against us' escalates violence.

with **Canon Margaret Sentamu, Bishop Kenneth Stevenson, Dr David Wilkinson.** *Closing Reflections by* **Dr Elaine Storkey.** *Introduced by* **Dr David Hope**

CAN WE BUILD A BETTER WORLD?

FIVE SESSIONS: Slavery – then and now; Friendship & Prayer – then and now; Change & Struggle – then and now; The Bible – then and now; Redemption & Restitution – then and now

We live in a divided and hurting world and with a burning question. As Christians in the 21st century how can we – together with others of good will – build a better world? Important material for important issues.

with **Archbishop John Sentamu, Wendy Craig, Leslie Griffiths. Five Poor Clares from BBC TV's The Convent.** *Introduced by* **Dr David Hope**

WHERE IS GOD...?

FIVE SESSIONS: Where is God when we ... seek happiness? ... face suffering? ... make decisions? ... contemplate death? ... try to make sense of life?

If we are to find honest answers to these big questions we need to undertake some serious and open thinking. Where better to do this than with trusted friends in a study group around this course?

with **Archbishop Rowan Williams, Patricia Routledge** CBE, **Joel Edwards, Dr Pauline Webb.** *Introduced by* **Dr David Hope**

BETTER TOGETHER?

FIVE SESSIONS: Family Relationships; Church Relationships; Relating to Strangers; Broken Relationships; Our Relationship with God

All about relationships – in the church and within family and society; building strong relationships and coping with broken ones. *Better Together?* looks frankly at how the Christian perspective may differ from that of society at large.

with **the Abbot of Ampleforth, John Bell, Nicky Gumbel, Jane Williams.** *Introduced by* **Dr David Hope**

TOUGH TALK
Hard Sayings of Jesus

FIVE SESSIONS: Shrinking and Growing; Giving and Using; Praying and Forgiving; Loving and Telling; Trusting and Entering

Looks at many of the hard sayings of Jesus in the Bible and faces them squarely. His uncomfortable words need to be faced if we are to allow the full impact of the gospel on our lives. *Tough Talk* is not for the faint-hearted.

with **Bishop Tom Wright, Steve Chalke, Fr Gerard Hughes SJ, Professor Frances Young.** *Introduced by* **Dr David Hope**

NEW WORLD, OLD FAITH

FIVE SESSIONS: Brave New World?; Environment and Ethics; Church and Family in Crisis?; One World – Many Faiths; Spirituality and Superstition

How does Christian faith continue to shed light on a range of issues in our changing world, including change itself? This course helps us make sense of our faith in God in today's world.

with Archbishop Rowan Williams, David Coffey, Joel Edwards, Revd Dr John Polkinghorne KBE FRS, Dr Pauline Webb. Introduced by Dr David Hope

IN THE WILDERNESS

FIVE SESSIONS: Jesus, Satan and the Angels; The Wilderness Today; The Church in the Wilderness; Prayer, Meditation and Scripture; Solitude, Friendship and Fellowship

Like Jesus, we all have wilderness experiences. What are we to make of these challenges and how are we to meet them? *In the Wilderness* explores these issues for our world, for the church, and at a personal level.

with Cardinal Cormac Murphy-O'Connor, Archbishop David Hope, Revd Dr Rob Frost, Roy Jenkins, Dr Elaine Storkey

FAITH IN THE FIRE

FIVE SESSIONS: Faith facing Facts; Faith facing Doubt; Faith facing Disaster; Faith fuelling Prayer; Faith fuelling Action

When things are going well our faith may remain untroubled, but what if doubt or disaster strike? Those who struggle with faith will find they are not alone.

with Archbishop David Hope, Rabbi Lionel Blue, Steve Chalke, Revd Dr Leslie Griffiths, Ann Widdecombe MP

JESUS REDISCOVERED

FIVE SESSIONS: Jesus' Life and Teaching; Following Jesus; Jesus: Saviour of the World; Jesus is Lord; Jesus and the Church

Re-discovering who Jesus was, what he taught, and what that means for his followers today. Several believers share what Jesus means to them.

with Paul Boateng MP, Dr Lavinia Byrne, Joel Edwards, Bishop Tom Wright, Archbishop David Hope

LIVE YOUR FAITH

SIX SESSIONS: The Key - Jesus; Prayer; The Community - the Church; The Dynamic - the Holy Spirit; The Bible; The Outcome - Service & Witness

Christianity isn't just about what we believe: it's about how we live. A course suitable for everyone; particularly good for enquirers and those in the early stages of their faith.

with Revd Dr Donald English, Lord Tonypandy, Fiona & Roy Castle

GREAT EVENTS, DEEP MEANINGS

SIX SESSIONS: Christmas; Ash Wednesday; Palm Sunday; Good Friday; Easter; Pentecost

Explains clearly what the feasts and fasts are about and challenges us to respond spiritually and practically. There are even a couple of quizzes to get stuck into!

with Revd Dr John Polkinghorne KBE FRS, Gordon Wilson, Bishop David Konstant, Fiona Castle, Dame Cicely Saunders, Archbishop David Hope

2 ADDITIONAL COURSES
ATTENDING, EXPLORING, ENGAGING

with **Archbishop David Hope, Steve Chalke, Fr Gerard Hughes SJ, Professor Frances Young**
FIVE SESSIONS: Attending to God; Attending to One Another; Exploring Our Faith; Engaging with the World in Service; Engaging with the World in Evangelism

CD CONVERSATIONS

Nobel Prize winner Sir John Houghton CBE, FRS was Professor of Atmospheric Physics at Oxford University. He is a world expert on global warming, its implications and remedies. In a wide-ranging conversation with Canon John Young, Sir John talks on this CD about "Why I believe in Climate Change" and "Why I believe in Jesus Christ".

1 CD	**£5.00**
Multipack of **5** CDs	**£10.00**
Multipack of **25** CDs	**£25.00**

SCIENCE AND CHRISTIAN FAITH

NOW ON CD

An in-depth discussion with the Revd Dr John Polkinghorne KBE FRS, former Professor of Mathematical Physics at Cambridge University.

CD/Audiotape	**£5.00**
Multipack of **5** CDs	**£10.00**
Multipack of **25** CDs	**£25.00**

BOOKS and BOOKLETS
ARCHBISHOP'S SCHOOL SERIES

7 BOOKLETS COMMISSIONED BY Dr DAVID HOPE – Prayer; Bible Reading; Evangelism; The Sacraments; Christianity and Science; Healing and Wholeness; Life After Death
Authors include John Polkinghorne & David Winter – 99p each
Special offer: You may order a complete set of all seven booklets for only £5

THE TEACHING OF JESUS

with **Steve Chalke, Professor James Dunn, Dr Pauline Webb, Archbishop David Hope**
FIVE SESSIONS: Forgiveness; God; Money; Heaven and Hell; On Being Human

Comprising photocopyable notes, audiotape and transcript

AUDIOTAPE: £8.99 *(£6.99 each for 5 or more)*
TRANSCRIPT: £4.99 *(£2.99 each for 2 or more)*
PHOTOCOPYABLE NOTES: **£2.99**

TOPIC TAPES
STRUGGLING/COPING
4 personal conversations

TAPE 1: **£5.00**
*Living with **depression**; Living with **panic attacks***
TAPE 2: **£5.00**   *(Set of 2 tapes **£8.50**)*
*Living with **cancer**; Living with **bereavement***

EVANGELISM TODAY   **£5.00**
with contributions by Canon Robin Gamble, the Revd Brian Hoare, Bishop Gavin Reid and Canon Robert Warren

FINDING FAITH   **£1.99**
is a 20-minute audiotape, designed for enquirers and church members. Four brief stories by people, including Archbishop David Hope, who have found faith.
Inexpensive! Designed as a 'give away'

PRAYER   **£3.50**
SIDE 1: Archbishop David Hope on *Prayer*
SIDE 2: Four Christians on praying ... for healing; in danger; in tongues; with perseverance
This tape accompanies the booklet
The Archbishop's School of Prayer

JOURNEYS INTO FAITH

A4 workbook for groups to encourage effective outreach
Was **£7.99** now **£1.50**

Published by *Churches Together in England* and *The Bible Society*

TEACH YOURSELF CHRISTIANITY **£9.99**

Fully revised in 2008 Hodder paperback, written by John Young, author of most of our course booklets.

YORK COURSES

York Courses · PO Box 343 · York YO19 5YB
Tel: **01904 466516** · Fax: **01904 630577** · email: courses@yorkcourses.co.uk
Visit www.yorkcourses.co.uk for the latest special offers and discounts plus secure online ordering. **ALL PRICES HELD UNTIL 1st AUGUST 2010.**
Payment with order please. Cheques: York Courses
FREE PACKING AND 2nd CLASS POSTAGE IN THE UK

VISA · DELTA · Maestro · EUROCARD MasterCard

The Brothers Karamazov. A wealthy landowner is out hunting with his hounds. A peasant's child comes into view. Just for the fun of it, the hunter turns his hounds on the child. This incident is too much for Ivan Karamazov. It makes him give up his belief in God.

Children on the cross

I think of each of these children as 'the child on the cross'. On page 5 there is a picture of such a child. The picture was taken in a war-zone – it doesn't matter which. He is a hungry boy. He's been strung up because he stole some food. That is his punishment. That picture of one hungry boy can stand for all those other 'children on a cross' – children on crosses because that is where, by our neglect or by our cruelty, we have put them.

We think of the cross as the means of salvation. 'He died that we might be forgiven.' That is true. Jesus died for us. That belongs to the bedrock of our faith. Christ died to save us; to set us free from our sin and guilt and to bring us home to God. True.

True – but not the whole truth. The cross is not only a path to heaven. The cross is rooted in our world and it is about our world. The cross is about that baby girl, thrown away like garbage. The cross is about Pintu, slaving among those stinking skins. The cross is about every child who suffers because of a grown-up's cruelty. Jesus said, 'Whoever receives one such child in my name receives me' (Mark 9.37). Whoever receives Pintu – or the unwanted and abandoned child, or the abused child – receives Jesus.

'Receive' in the New Testament is a rich word. It suggests hospitality, but it means opening your heart as well as your home to someone. Who was that little blind boy, who climbed me like a tree? What was his name? For Mother Teresa, he was the child Christ. That's who Pintu is. That's who that little girl, thrown into a bin, is. That's who every one of them is, every child who is the innocent victim of an adult's brutality.

When we see the image of a child hurting so badly we must superimpose upon it that other image – that of Christ on his cross. We bring the two images together so they become one. The image on page 5 perhaps helps us to do that. As Jesus was dying, he cried, 'I thirst' (John 19.28). But as we hear that cry, we hear too the thirsty child; the dehydrated child; the child wasting away for lack of clean water – while a grieving mother watches.

The sub-Saharan Jesus

'While a grieving mother watches'. Again, two images become one.

The first image is of the African mother, cradling her child who is dying of diarrhoea. The second image is of Mary at the foot of the cross, watching her child die. Tradition tells us that she too cradles his body, when it is brought down from the cross.

The two images become one. In a dry dusty village, south of the Sahara, far from the nearest water, Jesus son of Mary is wasting away while his mother watches. On an execution ground, on wasteland outside Jerusalem, beneath a sky turned black, slowly and painfully an African child expires.

For the mother somewhere in sub-Saharan Africa, at this very moment watching her little boy or girl slip away, and for Mary at the foot of the cross – for both mothers the words of Simeon come true: 'a sword will pierce your soul' (Luke 2.35).

Mary our mother

We stay with Mary a moment more. She is so alone – yet she is not altogether alone. Jesus commends his mother and his beloved disciple to each other: 'Woman, behold your son'. And to the disciple he loves: 'Behold your mother' (John 19. 26–27).

So they are called to support each other. But it is not a case of propping each other up in a world where there is nothing left to live for. There is work to be done. John will bear witness to what he has seen. He will tell us how it really was. 'The Word became flesh and dwelt among us' (John 1.14). He will recall his dear friend's words: 'And I, if I am lifted up from the earth, will draw all people to myself' (John 12.32).

And Mary? She fades from the scene, but she does not fade in significance. She is still Mother to the family of Jesus. We often speak of Pentecost as the birthday of the Church. But in truth it began long before that. The family of God is there beneath the cross. Mary and John – you and I – brought together *at* Calvary, brought together *by* Calvary. The death-throes of 'the child on the cross' are the birth-pangs of the Church.

When a child is ill, intellectually beyond reach, it still remains that this child can be prayed over, prayed about, held before God.

*Metropolitan
Anthony Bloom*

Young children have more fears and phobias than adults, and experience the emotion of them more intensely.

Anxiety Care

Jesus was not crucified on an altar between two candles, but on a cross between two thieves.

Lord George MacLeod

Korean Blessing

May the Christ who walks with wounded feet,
walk with us on the road.
May the Christ who serves with wounded hands
stretch out our hands to serve.
May the Christ who loves with the wounded heart
open our hearts to love.

QUESTIONS FOR GROUPS

BIBLE READING: Matthew 18.1–6, 10–14

1. **Read Luke 2.51–52.** Did you have a happy childhood? Select one especially happy incident and one unhappy incident to share. Do such memories help you to understand today's children? What are the big differences between growing up today and when group members were children?

2. A recent report suggested that many of Britain's children are unhappy. Many children suffer in the 'developing world'. What are the less obvious ways in which children suffer in more affluent countries, such as Britain?

3. **Read Mark 9.36–37.** In what practical ways, both at church and in your neighbourhood, does your congregation welcome Jesus by welcoming children? How might you do even better?

4. **Read Matthew 18.3.** What on earth does it mean for an adult to become a child? Then read the words of Sister Dominica in the box on page 14. How can we follow the example of those children by living in the 'now'?

5. **Read John 19.26–27.** What do these words say to us about the Christian understanding of family?

6. Spend 2 minutes looking at the picture in the booklet of 'the child on the cross' (p. 5). What thoughts come to mind? How can the Church – starting with your own church and (perhaps) this discussion group – begin to address the plight of 'the child on the cross'?

7. Are we called to carry the weight of the world's pain on our shoulders? In a world where so many children suffer, is there any place for joy, laughter, praise and singing? (John Bell's comment in the box on page 13 might help.)

8. The character Ivan in Dostoevsky's *The Brothers Karamazov* gave up his belief in God because of what one child went through. Does the experience of 'the child on the cross' make any difference to the way you think about God?

9. **Re-read Matthew 18.5–6.** What do you think Jesus meant by this? Given that many child-abusers were themselves abused as children, is society too harsh on them? How might your church show love and acceptance to them? Or would you prefer to keep them out altogether – away from children in your church?

10. **Read Exodus 20.12.** Britain has more over-60-year-olds than under-16s. Do churches place too much emphasis on children and young people? Most congregations have a lot of *older* people, but while many churches appoint a youth worker, very few appoint a worker for the elderly. What do you make of that?

11. In the violence which is war we often read of 'collateral damage'. Weasel words for killing the innocent, including children? Shouldn't all Christians be pacifists? But the West is criticised for not intervening in the Rwandan holocaust, and the Archbishop of York called for intervention in Zimbabwe. Can soldiers be peace-keepers, or is that a contradiction in terms?

12. In closing, think of some of the organisations known to you (at home and overseas) which care for and cater for children. Draw up a list and pray for these children and the organisers.

SESSION 4

OUTSIDE A CITY WALL

I have been indoors all my life, whilst you have battled for the Church in the world.

Cardinal Newman to Bishop Ullathorne

I'm more use outside the Church.

John Studzinski CBE, Christian, investment banker, & philanthropist.

Unless one has placed oneself on the side of the oppressed, to feel with them, one cannot understand.

Simone Weil

To understand why Jesus died – not that we ever fully can – we have to notice *when* he died and *how* he died and *where* he died.

When, how, and where?

When did Jesus die? All the Gospels agree that he died at the season of Passover. St John suggests that he died on the very day and at the very hour when the Passover lamb was sacrificed in the Temple. He was, as John the Baptist had announced, 'The Lamb of God who carries – and carries away – the sin of the world' (John 1.29). The wonderful feast of Passover, with its special food, ceremonies and songs, celebrates the deliverance of an enslaved people. Good Friday is nothing if it is not a festival of freedom. Perhaps the character in the Good Friday story who knew best what the day meant was Barabbas (Mark 15.6-15). He woke up expecting to die that day. Instead he walked free. Think what that day meant to him!

How did Jesus die? He was crucified. He was not, for example, stoned. Crucifixion was an excruciatingly cruel death. But the physical agony of it is not something the Gospels dwell on – unlike, say, Mel Gibson in his film *The Passion of the Christ*. What was significant was not the cruelty of his death. Many have died just as painfully, including all the countless others whom the Romans crucified.

What we must notice is that Jesus was 'hanged on a tree' (Acts 10.39). As Peter put it, 'He himself bore our sins in his own body on the tree' (1 Peter 2.24). Those who saw what happened knew their Bibles. They remembered one terrible text: 'Cursed is he who hangs on a tree' (Deuteronomy 21.23; Galatians 3.13). In the picture language of the Bible, to die strung up on a tree was the worst fate imaginable. Anyone who died this way was seen as utterly abandoned, abandoned both by humankind and by God. No wonder Jesus cried from the cross, 'My God, why have you forsaken me?' (Mark 15.34).

Where did Jesus die? He died 'outside'. He suffered, says the Bible, 'outside the gate' (Hebrews 13.12). The gates of the city closed on the one about to die, just as the door of the inn closed on the one about to be born.

Jesus the outsider

Jesus was born outside; he died outside; outside was where he spent his days. He had 'nowhere to lay his head' (Matthew 8.20). Jesus is never found 'inside', where it's safe and comfortable. Think of the groups of 'insiders' at the time of Jesus. Jesus did not belong to any of them. He was not one of the Pharisees, the sticklers for the rules. He was not an aristocratic Sadducee. He was not planning violent revolution with the Zealots. There was no party to protect him or to promote his cause.

Jesus was an outsider. He was an outsider himself, and one with the outsiders he moved among – those suffering from disfiguring diseases; the hated tax-collectors; those whom the pious wrote off as 'sinners'. All 'the last, the least, and the lost'. Jesus was one with all those outside the circles of power and influence, not least women and little children.

The contrast between 'inside' and 'outside' becomes very stark in the days leading to the cross. 'Christ outside' stands over against the scheming inner circles around Caiaphas, Pilate and Herod. And on Good Friday he perishes outside. It is to that wasteland, outside a city wall, that we – abandoning all our transitory securities – are summoned to follow him. 'Jesus also suffered outside the city gate...' says the great text, 'Let us then go to him outside the city gate and bear the abuse he endured' (Hebrews 13.12-14).

Where is Jesus, we wonder? We have to go outside and look for him.

The crazy king

Some say that *King Lear* is the greatest work of literature in the English language. Shakespeare's play tells the story of a vain and foolish king. King Lear loves all the fanfares and fine clothes and fawning adulation that go with being a king. But his two oldest daughters strip him of all these things and turn him out of doors. They drive him outside. And outside, outside on a barren heath, outside in an appalling storm, outside in the dark, he comes at last to his senses. In one Christian word, there, outside, he is *saved*.

King Lear goes outside. But he is not alone. Others are there, outside with him. His heart-broken court jester is at his side. Edgar, a victim of the power-struggles in Lear's palace, appears from a hole in the heath, disguised as a crazed and naked beggar. Then there is Lear's loyal servant Kent, whom Lear had angrily banished. Now in disguise, he is still attending his master.

So we have this little company, none quite himself or what he seems. Together, outside, they endure the worst the wilderness can do to them. What they suffer there turns out to be a kind of redemption. They are tender and generous to one another. Lear himself at last notices that most people don't live in luxury. His heart goes out to all the 'poor naked wretches' who, on such a night, have no roof over their heads.

What are we watching when we see this weird quartet out there in the storm on the heath? Who are they, this broken king and his companions? They are – though it is not the word Shakespeare uses – a kind of church.

The mind of Christ

It is of course all quite mad. To go outside into the rain is folly. It is definitely not 'good practice'. But Jesus consistently advocates just such ill-advised behaviour. Think of the crazy things he bids us do: 'Turn the other cheek'; 'Go the extra mile'; 'Lend without expecting repayment'; and so on. Such tomfoolery is impossible 'inside'. But for the community outside under the cross, love has its own new rules.

The call to be a Christian is in a deep sense a summons *outside*. In the language of the apostle Paul, it means not being 'conformed to this world' (Romans 12.2). That's to say, by the grace of God, our values and attitudes are no longer shaped by the prevailing culture. In the Western world, the culture that prevails is acquisitive, materialist, and competitive. It idolises 'celebrities'. It panders to greed. What you *have* matters more than what you *are*.

To join Jesus 'outside' is to allow ourselves to be moulded by the 'mind of Christ' instead of letting ourselves be shaped by how 'the world' thinks. Paul explains what this means in a wonderful passage in his letter to the Philippians (Philippians 2.5-11). There he says that the pattern of our thinking should be that of Jesus himself – the One who gave up his Father's glory, and life itself, to become one of us.

We are called, all of us, to join Jesus 'outside the city gate'. Some are called to obey that call in obvious ways. Earlier in this course we thought of monks and nuns, living their prayerful lives of silence and simplicity, far from the noisy confused world where the majority of us spend our days. Then there are those who are called by God to some form of full-time Christian service. They will have to settle for a path in life which will be unlikely to bring them material prosperity.

In the world but not of the world

But most of us are called to join Jesus 'outside' in less obvious ways. That call is just as demanding – perhaps more so. It is the call to be 'in the world but not of the world' (John 17.13-26). As Canon John Young wrote in an earlier York Course[1], 'Many an ordinary, apparently comfortable life has been offered to God, soaked in prayer, marked by faith, hospitality, forgiveness, good neighbourliness and sacrificial giving. This too is discipleship according to the New Testament.'

When I was on the staff of St Martin-in-the-Fields, we had a flat overlooking the courtyard around the church. At Christmas there was a crib in the courtyard. I remember, one Christmas morning, looking out of our flat window at that crib. Something strange had happened overnight. Baby Jesus had been turfed out of the crib. Curled up in the straw was one of London's many 'street homeless'.

As at his birth, so at his death, our Lord is outside. 'There is a green hill far away, outside a city wall.' Well, it wasn't a hill and, even though it was springtime, Golgotha certainly wasn't green. But it did happen outside. And whether I'm a monk in a monastery or a merchant banker with a mortgage, 'outside' is where I belong.

QUESTIONS FOR GROUPS
BIBLE READING: Mark 15.22–32; Hebrews 13.12–13

1. A Christian who runs a hostel for homeless men advises against giving money to street beggars. He knows that some of them peddle drugs. 'It's better to give to the Salvation Army.' A woman I know often asks street beggars if they'd like coffee and food. What is your practice?

2. **Read Luke 6.26.** In some parts of the world (Africa, China...) Christianity is popular and growing fast. But in modern Britain Christianity is increasingly marginalized – even despised by some. To be a Christian is to be an outsider. Do you feel the force of this? If so, does it bother you?

3. Feeling an outsider can be especially difficult for young people at school, college or work. How can we encourage young Christians to hold on to their Christian faith and values?

4. Some Christians feel that women will be 'outsiders' until the Church uses truly inclusive language and has a fully inclusive policy for ordination, including female bishops. Others feel that continuing to hold on to traditional views is now turning them into outsiders in their own Church. What do you think about this? (Christina Baxter's words may be helpful here – track [34] on CD/transcript).

5. 'We are a very friendly church.' Yet some churches neglect the visitor (the 'outsider') because members are so busy talking to their friends after the service. Mark your church 0–6 on a 'good at hospitality' scale (0 = poor; 6 = excellent).

   Note: John Bell makes some interesting comments on this (track [37] on CD/transcript).

6. ***Read Luke 19.1–10.*** With the help of Luke chapter 5, draw up a list of 'Gospel outsiders'. Each group member might choose one incident in the Gospels when Jesus meets an 'outsider'. Tell the story from your point of view. ('I want to tell you what I was doing up that sycamore tree' might be one way to start!)

7. On 'Back to Church Sunday' thousands of new faces appear in our churches, invited by friends. Draw up a list of people you might invite. How (if at all) would you want to modify your service on that day, to make 'outsiders' feel at home?

8. ***Read Matthew 27.55–56.*** The radically simple lifestyle of Jesus and his disciples depended on a 'back-up team'. Using your imagination, what might that have meant in practice? What are the issues raised here for modern Christians?

9. Archbishop William Temple was reported as saying that the Church is the one organisation which exists entirely for the benefit of non-members. Do you agree? If so, what are the practical implications for your group and for your church?

10. ***Read Matthew 18.20.*** Most churches have a lot of 'insider stuff' – committees, synods, buildings, rituals... Some radical Christians have said that we should abandon all that 'inside' paraphernalia. They say that we should find an upper room somewhere and start again. What do you think?

11. In our modern secular, superstitious and multi-faith society, should Britain continue to have laws which ensure an Anglican monarch and spouse, and bishops in the House of Lords?

12. ***Read Romans 12.1–2*** and the box at foot of page 17. 'Do not be conformed to this world...'. In what ways/at which points do Christian values cut across society's values?

13. Some churches have a remarkable ministry to those outside the Church e.g.
    • www.depaulnightstopuk.org
      Nightstop for homeless young people
    • www.streetpastors.org.uk
      street pastors in cities
    • www.skateboardersforchrist.org
      making skateboarders welcome – with their boards!
    • www.scumoftheearth.net
      The Scum of the Earth Church in Colorado.

    Group members with knowledge of these or other ministries to 'outsiders' are invited to share. You might wish to close this session by praying for them.

If *The Beatles* get on the side of Christ, which they always were, and let people know that, then maybe the churches won't be full, but there'll be a lot of Christians dancing in dance halls. Whatever they celebrate, God and Christ, I don't think it matters as long as they're aware of Him and His message.   *John Lennon*

---

[1] *Jesus Rediscovered* – see centre pages of this booklet

SESSION 5

YORK COURSES

WHEN I SURVEY...
Christ's cross and ours

A course in five sessions
written by John Pridmore
Accompanying CD tape and transcript available

Touching The Rock

> When I lay on rotting prison straw... it was disclosed to me that the line separating Good and Evil passes, not through States, not between classes, not between political parties either – but right through every human heart.
>
> *Alexander Solzhenitsyn*

> Death is not the end. Death is now the door into something which is far greater.
> *John Bell*

> I am not dying. I am entering into life.
> *St Thérèse of Lisieux (1873-1897)*

Calvary stands in many places. Wherever in the world sin and suffering have carved deep wounds, those wounds are in the shape of a cross. I think of the 'Gulag Archipelago' – that chain of labour camps across the frozen wastes of Siberia, to which the Soviet government consigned those they deemed enemies of the state. Millions perished. Calvary stood in the Gulag Archipelago.

The Russian writer Alexander Solzhenitsyn – one of the towering moral and spiritual giants of modern times – lived, and nearly died, in those camps. In his great book *The Gulag Archipelago* he writes of his time there. He tells how those camps robbed him of everything that makes life meaningful. He is robbed of his name – he is known only by a number. He is robbed of books and pen and paper – a dreadful deprivation for a writer of his stature. He is robbed of work he can do with dignity. Instead he must labour as a slave. He is deprived of sufficient food and sleep. He gets no letters. He hears no news of his family or of the outside world. He is stripped of his own clothes and dressed in verminous rags. He is robbed of his health – he succumbs to cancer.

Solzhenitsyn, robbed of everything, sinks as it were to the bottom, to the very base of being. And then he says something extraordinary. He writes of the day, 'when I deliberately let myself sink to the bottom and felt it firm under my feet – the hard rocky bottom which is the same for all.'

'I deliberately let myself sink to the bottom – *and I felt it firm under my feet.*' I cannot think of any words in modern literature that have moved me more than these.

Good Friday

At the last, on the Friday we call 'good', Jesus is brought to the bottom of the abyss. He too finds it firm under his feet. For his final words from the cross are not words of dereliction or of despair but of trust. 'Father, into your hands I commend my spirit' (Luke 23.46).

St Paul writes of Christ's descent into the depths.

> *Your attitude should be the same as that of Christ Jesus, who, being in the very nature of God, did not consider equality with God something to be grasped, but made himself nothing, taking the very nature of a servant, being made in human likeness. And being found in appearance as a man, he humbled himself and became obedient to death – even death on a cross.* (Philippians 2.5-8)

21

> When the flood recedes, the rock is there.
>
> *Chinese Proverb*

> He brought me up also out of a horrible pit, out of the miry clay, and set my feet upon a rock.
>
> *Psalm 40:2*

> Faith like Job's cannot be shaken because it is the result of having been shaken.
>
> *Rabbi Abraham Heschel*

> Although the world is full of suffering, it is full also of the overcoming of it.
>
> *Helen Keller*

> My barn having burned to the ground, I can now see the moon.
>
> *Japanese poet*

'Even death on a cross'. And even that perhaps was not the limit of his descent. He was brought lower still. 'The inner crucifixion' of Christ was what he suffered in heart and mind and spirit, beyond what he endured in his body. As the Apostles' Creed has it, 'He descended into hell'. The mystery of what this means is beyond our minds. But one thing we can say: wherever Christ's cross takes him, at the end he finds his Father there.

The Psalmist asks God, 'Where can I go from your Spirit? Where can I flee from your presence?' Then he answers his own question.

If I go up to the heavens, you are there; if I make my bed in hell, you are there. If I rise on the wings of the dawn, if I settle on the far side of the sea, even there your hand will guide me, your right hand will hold me fast. (Psalm 139.8-10).

God is there, says the Psalmist, 'even if I make my bed in hell'. Is that true? If it is true, there is hope for all those who – by their own fault, or by someone else's fault, or by no one's fault – 'make their bed in hell'. For there are those, some perhaps following this York Course, who have been there – there where Christ's cross took him.

Abba, Father

Jesus descends into hell and finds his Father there. And I hear someone say, 'Watch your language!' Now is not the time to discuss the rights and wrongs of calling God 'Father'. Many would say that there are more wrongs than rights in a word that makes God sound male. But if we stay with that word, it is not because of what it tells us about God's gender. We stay with that word because good fathers are *trustworthy*.

'Father, into your hands I commend my spirit.' Jesus, in the depths of the abyss he entered at Calvary, came to a place where trust was possible. Some say that the word Jesus actually used must have been *Abba*, the personal form of address that a child would use in talking to his or her father. That is how Jesus had prayed in the Garden of Gethsemane. '*Abba*, Father, if it be your will let this cup pass from me' (Mark 14.36). The cup did not pass from him. He drains it to its bitter dregs. But still he finds it possible to pray, '*Abba*, Father'. He touches the rock.

Touching the Rock

Over twenty years ago the educationalist John Hull became blind. *Touching the Rock* records his experience

> When we walk to the edge of all the light we have and take the step into the darkness of the unknown, we must believe that one of two things will happen. There will be something solid for us to stand on or we will be taught to fly.
>
> *Patrick Overton*

of what he lost – but also of what he found through the experience of losing his sight. He gave his book that title because he also came to a place where trust was possible – and wonder, too.

John writes of stepping out of his house into his front garden as the rain begins to fall. 'This is an experience of great beauty. I feel as if the world, which is veiled until I touch it, has suddenly disclosed itself to me. I feel that the rain is gracious, that it has granted a gift to me, the gift of the world.'

'Touching the rock'. When we are brought very low, so low that it seems we can sink no lower, we touch rock. That is what Alexander Solzhenitsyn and John Hull found to be true. That is what Jesus of Nazareth found to be true.

The traditional site of the crucifixion – as of the resurrection – is now covered by the Church of the Holy Sepulchre in Jerusalem. To reach the very place where they say Jesus died, you enter the church, turn right, and go up a short flight of stairs. You find yourself in a small chapel. There are icons and lots of candles. Against one wall is an altar, standing, it is said, over the exact point where the cross stood. Under the altar is a small hole in the floor of the chapel. Many pilgrims come here to pray. If you do what most of these pilgrims do, you will kneel before the altar, reach beneath it, and put your hand through that hole. If you do so, you will find yourself touching the rough hard cold surface of a bare rock.

Perhaps you are meeting in someone's sitting room – or maybe in a draughty church hall! In your imagination, join those pilgrims in the Church of the Holy Sepulchre. In your mind, kneel with them before that altar – and with them reach down to touch that rock.

Perhaps if we do that we shall catch a sense of something that our stupid words cannot begin to explain, a sense of what lies beneath all the confusions and contradictions of our mixed-up lives. Perhaps we shall 'touch the rock', the same rock that Christ touched in the dark place he went to for us.

So may we find, as our Saviour did, that 'the eternal God is our refuge and underneath are the everlasting arms' (Deuteronomy 33.27).

QUESTIONS FOR GROUPS

BIBLE READING: Psalm 139

1. Good Friday with its suffering, Holy Saturday with its waiting and Easter Sunday with its joy, all belong together. How do you like to keep Good Friday? Does the 'waiting' on the Saturday mean much to you?

2. **Read Luke 24.36–49.** What does Easter Sunday mean to you? And how do you like to celebrate it?

3. Re-read the paragraph on page 23 describing John Hull's loss of sight. Sit quietly and try to imagine his slow but inevitable journey into blindness – and his joy at feeling rain on his face. Group members are invited to share their own losses and any unexpected joys linked with these – and the significance of their faith in all this.

4. **Read Matthew 7.24–28.** After her Bible class, a teenager is required to ask older church members how they have built their lives on rock, and how she might do the same. If that question were put to you by a teenager – assuming you're no longer one yourself! – how would you respond?

5. **Luke 23.44–49.** Jesus' final saying from the cross is an affirmation of trust. 'Father, into your hands I commend my spirit.' Do group members think much about their own death? If so, where do these reflections take you? Do these words of Jesus help? You might find it helpful to consider comments by General Dannatt (track [45] on the CD/transcript) and John Bell's words in the box on page 21.

6. Read the box on page 23 which describes the way Rowan Williams tackled his demanding sermon in Uganda. You might like to discuss his approach. Imagine you are talking with one man on death row. What would you say to help him 'touch rock'?

7. Think of great wickedness which has made news headlines, e.g. Dr Harold Shipman; Robert Mugabe. Is anyone beyond the redemptive love of God?

8. You might want to discuss future plans for your group – a social event, disband, another course perhaps, an outreach supper with a speaker ...

9. **Read Psalm 95.1–7.** Your group leader might give a pebble to each group member – or even bring in one large rock. Feel its texture and solidity. Imagine that you are pilgrims in the Church of the Holy Sepulchre in Jerusalem, kneeling to touch the rock where the cross stood (page 23). Afterwards, share what came to mind.

10. Raise any points from the course booklet or CD/audiotape which haven't been covered by your group, but which you would like to discuss.

11. Read the final sentence in Session 5. Sit quietly and reflect on those lovely words which end our course. Share what they mean to you – or what you hope they will come to mean to you – in the ups and downs of daily life.

> So we have reached the end of our journey, and we have arrived at no pleasant place. It is in fact a place of public execution. Yet all human roads lead here in the end. This is the capital of the kingdom of free men and there, ruling from the gallows, is the King.
>
> *G. Kitson Clark*